Overcoming Procrastination: A Step-by-Step Guide

1. --

2. Summary

3. Chapter 2

4. Chapter 1: Understanding Procrastination

5. Chapter 2: The Impact of Procrastination

6. Chapter 3: Identifying Your Procrastination Patterns

7. Chapter 4: Setting the Foundation for Change

8. Chapter 5: Time Management Strategies

9. Chapter 6: Cognitive Behavioral Techniques for Procrastinator

10. Chapter 7: Motivation and Reward Systems

11. Chapter 8: Breaking Down Tasks into Manageable Steps

12. Chapter 9: Developing Resilience Against Procrastination

13. Chapter 10: Technology and Tools to Combat Procrastination

14. Chapter 11: Creating a Supportive Environment

15. Chapter 12: Sustaining Progress and Preventing Relapse

16. Synopsis

Summary

Chapter 1: Understanding Procrastination 3

1.1 The Psychology Behind Procrastination 3

1.2 Fear of Failure and Perfectionism 5

1.3 Lack of Motivation: Causes and Effects 7

Chapter 2: The Impact of Procrastination 9

2.1 Personal Consequences 9

2.2 Professional Setbacks 1

2.3 Academic Challenges 1

Chapter 3: Identifying Your Procrastination Patterns 1

3.1 Recognizing Triggers and Habits 1

3.2 Self-Assessment Tools and Techniques 1

3.3 Creating a Personalized Procrastination Profile 1

Chapter 4: Setting the Foundation for Change 2

4.1 Goal Setting Principles 2

4.2 Prioritization Techniques 2

4.3 Establishing Realistic Deadlines 2

Chapter 5: Time Management Strategies 2

5.1 The Pomodoro Technique 2

5.2 Effective Scheduling Methods 2

5.3 Overcoming Distractions 3

Chapter 6: Cognitive Behavioral Techniques for Procrastinators 3

6.1 Challenging Negative Thoughts 3

6.2 Building a Positive Mindset 3

6.3 Visualization and Affirmation Practices 3

Chapter 7: Motivation and Reward Systems

7.1 Understanding Intrinsic vs Extrinsic Motivation

7.2 Designing Effective Reward Systems

7.3 Maintaining Long-Term Motivation

Chapter 8: Breaking Down Tasks into Manageable Steps

8.1 The Art of Task Segmentation

8.2 Using Micro-Goals for Macro Success

8.3 Dealing with Overwhelming Projects

Chapter 9: Developing Resilience Against Procrastination

9.1 Embracing Imperfection

9.2 Learning from Setbacks

9.3 Cultivating Grit and Determination

Chapter 10: Technology and Tools to Combat Procrastination

10.1 Digital Tools for Time Management

10.2 Apps for Focus and Productivity

10.3 Blocking Distractions in the Digital Age

Chapter 11: Creating a Supportive Environment

11.1 Building Accountability Partnerships

11.2 Seeking Professional Help When Needed

11.3 Fostering a Community of Productivity

Chapter 12: Sustaining Progress and Preventing Relapse

12.1 Monitoring Progress Through Journaling

12.2 Adjusting Strategies as Needed

12.3 Celebrating Milestones

1 Understanding Procrastination

1.1 The Psychology Behind Procrastination

Understanding the psychology behind procrastination is crucial for anyone looking to overcome this pervasive issue. At its core, procrastination is not merely a matter of poor time management or laziness, but rather a complex psychological behavior that involves the interplay of various emotional and cognitive factors. This exploration delves into the reasons why individuals may find themselves repeatedly postponing tasks, despite knowing the potential negative consequences.

One primary psychological factor behind procrastination is the fear of failure. Many individuals delay starting or completing tasks due to a deep-seated fear that their efforts will not result in success. This fear can be so overwhelming that avoiding the task altogether feels like a safer option than facing possible failure. Another closely related factor is perfectionism. Perfectionists often procrastinate because they have an all-or-nothing approach to tasks; if they cannot do something perfectly, they prefer not to do it at all. This mindset leads to a cycle of delay and stress as deadlines approach.

Lack of motivation also plays a significant role in procrastination. When individuals are not intrinsically motivated by the task at hand or do not see its immediate value, they are more likely to put it off in favor of activities that provide instant gratification. Additionally, decision paralysis can contribute to procrastination; when faced with too many choices or overwhelming tasks, people may freeze up and choose to do nothing instead.

Emotional regulation difficulties are another critical aspect of the psychology behind procrastination. Some individuals use procrastination as a coping mechanism to deal with negative emotions associated with a task, such as boredom, anxiety, or insecurity. By delaying the task, they temporarily avoid these unpleasant feelings but at the cost of increased stress and anxiety as deadlines loom closer.

In conclusion, understanding these psychological underpinnings is essential for addressing and overcoming procrastination effectively. Recognizing that procrastination is more about managing emotions than managing time allows individuals to adopt strategies that address these root causes directly. By tackling fear of failure, perfectionism, lack of motivation, decision paralysis, and emotional regulation difficulties head-on, one can begin to break the cycle of procrastination and move towards greater productivity and success.

1.2 Fear of Failure and Perfectionism

The intricate relationship between fear of failure and perfectionism plays a pivotal role in the psychology of procrastination. Understanding this dynamic is essential for anyone seeking to address procrastination at its roots. Fear of failure is not just about the dread of not achieving success; it deeply intertwined with our self-esteem and how we perceive our value in various aspects of life, including academic, professional, and personal spheres.

Perfectionism exacerbates this fear by setting an impossibly high bar for success. Perfectionists often believe that anything less than perfect is unacceptable, leading to a paralyzing fear of starting or completing tasks. This mindset creates a vicious cycle where the fear of failing to meet these unrealistic standards results in delaying or avoiding tasks altogether. The rony here is that procrastination, driven by perfectionism and fear of ailure, often leads to lower quality outcomes due to rushed work or missed pportunities, reinforcing the very fears that triggered the behavior.

Moreover, perfectionism isn't solely about high standards; it's also haracterized by a critical self-evaluation process. Perfectionists tend to be heir own harshest critics, focusing on flaws and mistakes rather than chievements and progress. This critical inner voice can lead to significant motional distress, including feelings of inadequacy and worthlessness hen perceived expectations are not met.

Understanding the root causes: Recognizing that both fear of failure and erfectionism stem from deeper psychological issues such as low self-steem or past experiences.

Challenging unrealistic standards: Actively working to redefine what uccess means on a more realistic scale can help mitigate the pressures that rive procrastination.

Developing healthier coping mechanisms: Learning to manage stress and nxiety without resorting to avoidance can help break the cycle of rocrastination.

In conclusion, addressing fear of failure and perfectionism requires a ultifaceted approach that includes self-reflection, changing thought atterns, and developing new behaviors. By understanding how these actors contribute to procrastination, individuals can begin taking steps owards overcoming this debilitating habit. It involves moving away from ll-or-nothing thinking patterns towards embracing imperfection as part of he human experience.

1.3 Lack of Motivation: Causes and Effects

Lack of motivation is a significant barrier to overcoming procrastination, deeply affecting an individual's ability to start or complete tasks. This phenomenon can stem from various sources, each intertwining with personal, professional, and academic aspects of life. Understanding the causes and effects of a lack of motivation is crucial for addressing procrastination effectively.

One primary cause of diminished motivation is the absence of clear goals or objectives. Without a specific target or purpose, tasks can seem meaningless, leading to disinterest and apathy. This scenario often results in procrastination as individuals struggle to find a compelling reason to engage with their responsibilities.

Another significant factor is the fear of failure, closely related to perfectionism as discussed previously. When individuals doubt their abilities or the possibility of achieving success, they may avoid starting tasks altogether. This avoidance behavior is a protective mechanism against potential failure and the associated negative emotions such as embarrassment or disappointment.

External factors also play a critical role in influencing motivation levels. A lackluster environment lacking stimulation or support can contribute to feelings of demotivation. Similarly, if individuals do not perceive their efforts as being recognized or rewarded appropriately, their drive to perform can significantly wane.

The effects of low motivation are far-reaching and can perpetuate a cycle of procrastination. Initially, it leads to delayed task initiation and completion, which often results in rushed work under pressure. This hurried approach typically lowers the quality of outcomes, reinforcing feelings of inadequacy and further diminishing motivation in a vicious cycle.

Beyond impacting task performance, chronic lack of motivation can have profound psychological effects. It may lead to decreased self-esteem as individuals question their capabilities and worth based on their perceived productivity failures. Moreover, this state can escalate into more severe mental health issues such as depression and anxiety if left unaddressed.

In conclusion, tackling lack of motivation requires a multifaceted strategy that addresses both intrinsic and extrinsic factors contributing to this state. By setting clear goals, fostering supportive environments, recognizing achievements, and managing fears around failure and perfectionism, individuals can begin to break the cycle of procrastination driven by motivational deficits.

2 The Impact of Procrastination

2.1 Personal Consequences of Procrastination

The personal consequences of procrastination are far-reaching and can significantly impact an individual's life in various detrimental ways. While the act of postponing tasks might seem harmless in the short term, its long-term effects can lead to a cascade of negative outcomes, affecting one's mental health, professional development, and personal relationships.

One of the most immediate and noticeable impacts of procrastination is on mental health. Chronic procrastinators often experience increased levels of stress and anxiety, stemming from the constant pressure of unfinished tasks looming over their heads. This perpetual state of stress can lead to more severe issues such as depression and burnout, particularly when individuals feel overwhelmed by their inability to meet deadlines or manage their responsibilities effectively.

Beyond mental health, procrastination can severely hinder professional growth and academic achievement. In a professional setting, delaying important tasks can result in missed opportunities, poor performance reviews, and even job loss. For students, habitual procrastination leads to cramming for exams and rushing assignments, which compromises the quality of work and ultimately affects grades and academic standing. The cycle of delay and last-minute panic undermines the development of essential skills such as time management, organization, and self-discipline —skills that are critical for success in both academic and professional arenas.

Procrastination also takes a toll on personal relationships. Friends, family members, and colleagues may perceive chronic procrastinators as unreliable r indifferent due to their consistent failure to follow through on commitments or meet shared responsibilities. This perception can strain relationships, leading to feelings of guilt and isolation among those who procrastinate.

Increased stress and anxiety due to constant pressure from unfinished asks

Negative impact on professional development through missed opportunities and poor performance

Deterioration of academic achievement as a result of cramming and rushed assignments

Strain on personal relationships due to perceived unreliability or indifference

In conclusion, while procrastination might offer temporary relief from immediate tasks or decisions, its long-term consequences are profoundly damaging across various aspects of an individual's life. Understanding these impacts is crucial for recognizing the importance of addressing procrastination head-on through effective strategies aimed at fostering productivity and well-being.

2.2 Professional Setbacks

The ramifications of procrastination in the professional sphere are both profound and multifaceted, extending far beyond mere missed deadlines. This behavior pattern can precipitate a series of setbacks that not only hinder an individual's career progression but can also tarnish their professional reputation. Understanding the depth and breadth of these consequences is crucial for comprehending the full impact of procrastination on one's professional life.

At its core, procrastination affects productivity, a key metric in any professional setting. The delay in completing tasks compromises the quality of work produced, as last-minute efforts rarely match the outcomes of well-planned projects. This decline in work quality can lead to poor performance reviews, which are often considered during promotions or salary increments, thereby directly impacting an individual's career advancement opportunities.

Beyond personal productivity and growth, procrastination can strain workplace relationships and teamwork dynamics. When tasks are delayed, it not only affects the individual responsible but also has a ripple effect on colleagues who may depend on that work to progress with their own responsibilities. This can lead to frustration and resentment within teams, eroding trust and collaboration—essential components for a harmonious and efficient working environment.

Moreover, chronic procrastination may label an individual as unreliable or uncommitted in the eyes of both peers and superiors. Such perceptions can be particularly damaging in professions where reputation and trustworthiness are paramount. Once established, these labels are difficult to shed and can limit networking opportunities, mentorship prospects, and even job security.

In extreme cases, consistent failure to meet deadlines or achieve targets due to procrastination can result in job loss. The termination of employment not only has immediate financial repercussions but also long-term career implications. Finding new employment becomes challenging when past performance issues related to procrastination come to light during reference checks.

In conclusion, while procrastination might seem like a minor habit of delaying tasks, its impact on one's professional life is significant and far-reaching. It hampers personal growth, undermines team dynamics, damages reputations, and jeopardizes employment stability—highlighting the importance of addressing this behavior through effective time management strategies and self-discipline techniques.

2.3 Academic Challenges

The academic journey is often fraught with various challenges, many of which are exacerbated by the habit of procrastination. This behavior significantly impacts students' ability to manage their time effectively, leading to a cascade of negative outcomes that can hinder their educational progress and overall academic experience.

One of the most immediate effects of procrastination in an academic setting is the decline in the quality of work submitted by students. Assignments completed in haste lack depth, research, and critical analysis, resulting in lower grades. Over time, this pattern can severely affect a student's GPA, limiting opportunities for scholarships, internships, and even admission into competitive programs or institutions for further education.

Beyond impacting grades and academic standing, procrastination also contributes to increased stress and anxiety levels among students. The cycle of delaying work until the last minute creates a perpetual state of catch-up, where students are constantly under pressure to complete assignments or prepare for exams. This heightened stress can lead to burnout, mental health issues, and a decrease in overall well-being.

Furthermore, procrastination undermines the development of essential life skills such as time management, organization, and self-discipline. These skills are crucial not only for academic success but also for personal growth and future professional endeavors. Students who habitually postpone tasks may find it challenging to adapt to environments that demand high levels o self-regulation and accountability.

In addition to individual consequences, procrastination can strain relationships with peers and educators. Group projects become particularly problematic when one or more members delay their contributions, potentially jeopardizing the group's dynamics and success. Moreover, educators may perceive chronic procrastinators as disinterested or unmotivated learners, which could influence their willingness to provide additional support or opportunities for engagement.

In conclusion, while procrastination might seem like a benign tendency to delay tasks temporarily, its impact on students' academic lives is profound and multifaceted. It affects not only their current educational achievements but also their future prospects and personal development. Addressing this issue requires concerted efforts from both individuals and educational institutions to foster environments that encourage timely task completion through effective strategies for motivation and time management.

3 Identifying Your Procrastination Pattern

3.1 Recognizing Triggers and Habits

Understanding the triggers and habits that lead to procrastination is crucial for anyone looking to overcome this barrier to success. Recognizing these patterns is the first step in developing strategies to counteract them, enabling individuals to enhance their productivity and achieve their goals. This section delves into the common triggers of procrastination, explores the habitual responses that often follow, and provides insights into breaking these cycles.

Procrastination triggers are varied and can be deeply personal, but they often include fear of failure, overwhelming tasks, lack of interest, or a perceived lack of skills. For many, the mere thought of starting a task that seems daunting or unenjoyable can trigger a procrastinatory response. This might manifest as seeking out distractions, rationalizing delays with excuses, or switching focus to less important tasks that are easier or more enjoyable.

Habits play a significant role in perpetuating procrastination. Once an individual responds to a trigger by delaying work on a task, this behavior can quickly become a default response. Over time, this cycle of trigger and response strengthens until procrastination becomes a deeply ingrained habit. Breaking free from this cycle requires not only recognizing the triggers but also understanding the habitual responses they evoke.

Ultimately, recognizing and addressing your unique triggers and habits is a personalized process that may involve trial and error. By remaining patient and persistent in identifying what specifically leads you to procrastinate—and experimenting with different strategies to break these patterns—you can develop a more productive approach to managing your time and achieving your objectives.

To combat these patterns, it's essential to develop new habits that promote action over delay. Strategies might include breaking tasks into smaller, more manageable parts to reduce overwhelm; setting clear deadlines and rewards for completion; changing your environment to minimize distractions; or seeking support from peers or mentors who can hold you accountable. Additionally, reframing how you think about tasks—focusing on positive outcomes rather than potential challenges—can help shift your mindset from avoidance to action

3.2 Self-Assessment Tools and Techniques

Identifying personal procrastination patterns is a pivotal step towards developing effective strategies for overcoming procrastination. This process begins with self-assessment, a critical examination of one's habits, triggers, and responses. Through the use of various tools and techniques, individuals can gain insights into their procrastination behaviors, enabling them to devise targeted interventions.

Self-assessment tools vary widely but often include questionnaires, journals, and digital tracking apps. Questionnaires are designed to help individuals reflect on their procrastination tendencies, identifying specific areas where they struggle the most. These might cover aspects such as time management, fear of failure, perfectionism, or task aversion. By answering honestly, individuals can pinpoint their primary procrastination triggers.

Journals offer another avenue for self-assessment. By keeping a daily or weekly log of tasks, along with any procrastination episodes and their triggers, individuals can begin to see patterns in their behavior. This method not only highlights when and how often procrastination occurs but also sheds light on the emotional or situational contexts that contribute to it. Over time, journaling can reveal deeply ingrained habits that may require attention.

Digital tracking apps represent a modern approach to self-assessment. These apps can monitor time spent on various activities throughout the day, providing users with concrete data on how they allocate their time. Some apps also allow users to set goals and track progress towards them, offering insights into both productive periods and times of delay.

Beyond these tools, reflection techniques such as mindfulness meditation can also play a role in self-assessment. Mindfulness encourages present-moment awareness without judgment, allowing individuals to observe their thoughts and feelings around procrastination more objectively. This heightened awareness can make it easier to recognize triggers as they occur in real-time.

In conclusion, self-assessment is an ongoing process that requires commitment and honesty. By utilizing a combination of tools and techniques tailored to their needs, individuals can uncover the root causes of their procrastination patterns. With this understanding in hand, they are better equipped to implement effective strategies for change.

3.3 Creating a Personalized Procrastination Profile

The journey to overcoming procrastination begins with a deep dive into one's own procrastination patterns, necessitating the creation of a personalized procrastination profile. This profile serves as a comprehensive map of an individual's unique procrastination habits, including triggers, behaviors, and consequences. By assembling this profile, individuals can tailor their strategies for combating procrastination to fit their specific needs, increasing the likelihood of success.

To start building this profile, individuals should first revisit the insights gained from self-assessment tools and techniques discussed previously. Questionnaires might have highlighted particular areas of struggle such as fear of failure or perfectionism, while journals could reveal patterns in timing or emotional states linked to procrastination episodes. Digital tracking apps offer concrete data on how time is spent, further enriching this profile.

Next, it's crucial to identify the emotional and cognitive responses that accompany procrastination. For many, procrastination is not just about delaying tasks but also involves experiencing feelings of guilt, anxiety, or even relief in the short term. Recognizing these emotions is key to understanding the full impact of procrastination on one's life and well-being.

Another important component is acknowledging the consequences of procrastination. These can range from missed deadlines and opportunities to strained relationships and reduced self-esteem. By clearly outlining these outcomes within the profile, individuals can confront the reality of their behavior's impact more directly.

Reflect on feedback from questionnaires to pinpoint specific problem areas.

Analyze journal entries for patterns in behavior and triggers.

Review data from digital tracking apps for insights into time management issues.

Acknowledge emotional responses related to procrastinating behaviors.

List down tangible consequences experienced due to procrastination.

In conclusion, creating a personalized procrastination profile is an essential step towards developing effective coping strategies. This tailored approach allows for interventions that are specifically designed to address an individual's unique challenges with procrastination. With this detailed understanding in hand, individuals are better equipped to make meaningful changes that support productivity and personal growth.

4 Setting the Foundation for Change

4.1 Goal Setting Principles

The journey to overcoming procrastination is significantly influenced by the principles of goal setting. Effective goal setting acts as a compass, guiding individuals through the fog of daily distractions and towards their desired outcomes. Understanding and applying these principles can transform an overwhelming task into manageable steps, thereby reducing the urge to procrastinate.

Firstly, it's essential to recognize the importance of specificity in goal setting. Vague goals contribute to procrastination because they lack clarity and direction, making it difficult for individuals to know where to start or when they have achieved their objective. Specific goals, on the other hand, provide a clear target and criteria for success, which enhances motivation and focus.

Another critical principle is the establishment of measurable goals. Measurability allows for tracking progress, which can be incredibly motivating. It enables individuals to see how far they have come and how close they are to achieving their goal, providing a sense of accomplishment that fuels further action.

Achievability is also paramount in goal setting. Goals should stretch an individual's abilities but remain within reach. Unrealistic goals can lead to frustration and increased procrastination due to fear of failure or overwhelm. Setting achievable goals ensures that individuals remain engaged and confident in their ability to succeed.

Relevance plays a crucial role as well. Goals should align with personal values and long-term objectives because when people work towards something that matters deeply to them, their intrinsic motivation increases. This alignment makes it easier to prioritize tasks and resist the temptation t procrastinate.

Lastly, time-bound goals introduce urgency and help prevent procrastination by creating a deadline for achievement. Without a specific timeframe, there's always the risk of postponing tasks indefinitely under th guise of "someday." Time constraints encourage planning and consistent effort over time.

Incorporating these principles into goal setting not only aids in overcoming procrastination but also enhances overall productivity and satisfaction with one's progress. By setting specific, measurable, achievable, relevant, and time-bound (SMART) goals, individuals can create a structured path forward that minimizes uncertainty and maximizes efficiency.

4.2 Prioritization Techniques

Prioritization stands as a critical bridge between goal setting and actual execution. While the principles of goal setting lay the groundwork for wha one aims to achieve, prioritization techniques determine the order and importance of tasks, ensuring that efforts are focused on what truly matters This section delves into various prioritization methods that can be applied to both personal and professional contexts, offering insights into how they can be effectively utilized to enhance productivity and drive meaningful progress.

The Eisenhower Matrix, also known as the Urgent-Important Matrix, is powerful tool for categorizing tasks based on their urgency and importance It helps in distinguishing between tasks that require immediate attention from those that are important but not urgent, allowing individuals to focus on activities that contribute significantly to their long-term goals.

Another effective technique is the Pareto Principle or the 80/20 rule, which posits that 80% of results come from 20% of efforts. Applying this principle involves identifying the tasks or activities that will yield the most significant outcomes and allocating resources accordingly. This approach encourages efficiency by focusing on high-impact tasks rather than spreading oneself too thin across numerous less impactful ones.

Additionally, the ABCDE method offers a straightforward way to prioritize tasks by assigning them letters based on their importance and urgency. 'A' represents tasks of utmost priority, while 'E' denotes items of minimal importance. This method simplifies decision-making by providing a clear hierarchy of task importance.

The Eisenhower Matrix: Differentiating between urgent and important tasks.

The Pareto Principle: Focusing on tasks with the highest impact.

The ABCDE Method: Assigning priority levels to tasks for better organization.

Incorporating these prioritization techniques into daily routines can significantly enhance one's ability to manage time effectively, reduce stress by avoiding last-minute rushes, and ensure progress towards achieving set goals. By understanding and applying these methods, individuals can create a structured approach to tackling their workload, leading to improved productivity and satisfaction with their accomplishments.

4.3 Establishing Realistic Deadlines

Establishing realistic deadlines is a pivotal aspect of project management and personal productivity that directly follows the prioritization of tasks. It serves as a crucial step in translating prioritized tasks into actionable plans. This process involves setting time frames that are challenging yet achievable, taking into account various factors such as task complexity, available resources, and potential obstacles. The ability to set realistic deadlines is instrumental in ensuring timely progress while maintaining high standards of quality and minimizing stress.

One fundamental principle in establishing realistic deadlines is understanding the scope and requirements of each task or project. This involves a detailed analysis of the work involved, breaking down larger projects into smaller, manageable tasks, and assessing each for its time requirements. Additionally, it's important to consider the individual or team's capacity and other concurrent commitments to avoid overloading an ensure a balanced distribution of work.

Another critical factor is incorporating buffers for unexpected delays or challenges. While optimism is valuable, realism ensures that deadlines are not just aspirational but attainable. Including buffer times allows for flexibility and adaptability when unforeseen circumstances arise, reducing the need for drastic adjustments or compromises on quality.

Risk assessment plays a significant role in setting realistic deadlines. Identifying potential risks early on—such as resource shortages, technical difficulties, or dependencies on external factors—enables proactive planning to mitigate these risks or adjust timelines accordingly.

Communication is also key in establishing effective deadlines. Engaging with all stakeholders—including team members, clients, and suppliers—to gather insights and align expectations ensures that deadlines are agreed upon collectively and are more likely to be committed to by all parties involved.

In conclusion, establishing realistic deadlines requires a comprehensive approach that includes understanding task requirements, assessing capacities and risks, incorporating buffers for flexibility, and ensuring clear communication among stakeholders. By adhering to these principles, individuals and teams can set themselves up for success, achieving their goals efficiently while maintaining well-being and motivation.

5 Time Management Strategies

5.1 The Pomodoro Technique

In the quest to conquer procrastination and enhance productivity, the Pomodoro Technique emerges as a remarkably simple yet effective time management method. Developed in the late 1980s by Francesco Cirillo, this technique has gained widespread popularity among students, professionals, and anyone looking to improve their focus and efficiency. The core principle of the Pomodoro Technique is to break work into short, timed intervals known as "Pomodoros," traditionally 25 minutes in length, followed by a short break.

The beauty of the Pomodoro Technique lies in its simplicity and adaptability. By dividing work into manageable chunks, individuals can tackle tasks with greater focus and less intimidation. This approach not only helps in maintaining concentration but also significantly reduces the urge to procrastinate. Each Pomodoro session demands undivided attention to the task at hand, creating a sense of urgency that propels one forward. After each session, a brief break provides an essential respite, allowing for mental recovery before diving into the next focused interval.

Implementing the Pomodoro Technique requires nothing more than a timer and a list of tasks. The process begins with selecting a task, setting the timer for 25 minutes, and working on the task until the timer rings. Following this concentrated effort, a short break of about five minutes is taken. This cycle repeats three more times before taking a longer break of 15-30 minutes after completing four Pomodoros. This rhythm caters to our natural workflow and cognitive limits while preventing burnout.

In conclusion, the Pomodoro Technique stands out as an invaluable tool for anyone seeking to combat procrastination and elevate their productivity levels. Its straightforward framework complements various working styles and preferences, making it an adaptable strategy for achieving sustained focus and efficiency.

Enhances focus by limiting distractions during each Pomodoro

Improves time estimation for tasks through repeated cycles

Encourages regular breaks to maintain high levels of mental performance

Creates a sense of accomplishment that fuels motivation

The effectiveness of the Pomodoro Technique extends beyond mere time management; it fosters an environment where work becomes less overwhelming and more structured. By breaking down tasks into discrete intervals, individuals can monitor progress in real-time and adjust their strategies accordingly. Moreover, this technique cultivates discipline in managing distractions—a critical skill in today's information-saturated world.

5.2 Effective Scheduling Methods

In the realm of time management, effective scheduling stands as a cornerstone for achieving both short-term tasks and long-term goals. While the Pomodoro Technique offers a structured approach to managing individual tasks with focused intervals, broader scheduling methods are essential for integrating these tasks into a cohesive plan. Effective scheduling methods not only encompass the allocation of specific time slots for tasks but also require an understanding of one's energy levels, priorities, and the inevitable interferences that daily life presents.

One fundamental aspect of effective scheduling is the prioritization of tasks based on their urgency and importance. This can be visualized through tools like the Eisenhower Matrix, which categorizes tasks into four quadrants: urgent and important, important but not urgent, urgent but not important, and neither urgent nor important. By identifying where each task falls within this matrix, individuals can make informed decisions about what to focus on during their most productive hours.

Another key method involves time blocking or calendar blocking, where large blocks of time are dedicated to specific categories of activities or single tasks. This method goes beyond mere to-do lists by assigning a 'when' and 'how long' to each task, transforming intentions into scheduled appointments with oneself. Time blocking can be particularly effective when combined with thematic days, where each day of the week is dedicated to a particular type of work or activity, thus providing clear focus areas without daily decision fatigue.

Moreover, understanding one's biological prime time – the time of day when one is most alert and productive – allows for the scheduling of high-priority or intellectually demanding tasks during these peak periods. Conversely, less demanding or routine tasks can be scheduled during off-peak times.

Lastly, flexibility within a schedule is crucial. Life's unpredictability means that rigid schedules often lead to frustration rather than productivity. Incorporating buffer times between scheduled blocks allows for adjustment due to unforeseen circumstances or opportunities for rest.

In conclusion, while techniques like the Pomodoro offer micro-level task management strategies, effective scheduling on a macro level requires a holistic view that considers priorities, personal rhythms, and adaptability.

By employing methods such as prioritization matrices, time blocking with thematic days, aligning tasks with biological prime times, and allowing for flexibility in planning; individuals can create personalized schedules that enhance productivity while maintaining balance.

5.3 Overcoming Distractions

In the journey toward effective time management, overcoming distractions emerges as a pivotal challenge that can significantly impact one's ability to execute scheduled tasks and achieve goals. Distractions come in various forms, from digital notifications to environmental noise, and personal habits, each requiring a tailored strategy for mitigation. Understanding and implementing techniques to minimize or eliminate these distractions is crucial for maintaining focus and productivity.

One of the first steps in overcoming distractions is identifying their sources. Digital distractions, such as social media notifications, emails, and instant messages, are among the most common disruptors of focus in today's connected world. Creating a designated workspace that minimizes environmental distractions is also essential. This space should be organized and reserved for work or study only, helping to cue your brain into focusing when you're in that area.

Implementing technology wisely can play a significant role in managing digital interruptions. Tools like website blockers or apps that limit screen time on specific platforms during work hours can help maintain focus. Moreover, setting specific times to check emails or messages rather than responding to them impulsively can reduce the constant switching between tasks that hampers productivity.

Another effective strategy involves scheduling breaks intentionally throughout the day. Techniques like the Pomodoro Technique not only structure work into focused intervals but also incorporate short breaks to prevent burnout and maintain high levels of concentration throughout each work period. These breaks can also serve as an allocated time for checking personal devices, thus limiting the urge to do so during focused work sessions.

Personal habits play a significant role in how susceptible one is to distractions. Developing self-discipline through mindfulness practices or meditation can enhance one's ability to recognize when they are becoming distracted and gently guide their focus back to the task at hand without harsh self-judgment.

In conclusion, overcoming distractions requires a multifaceted approach that includes creating an optimal environment for focus, utilizing technology judiciously, managing personal habits, and incorporating structured breaks into one's schedule. By addressing these areas proactively, individuals can significantly improve their productivity and efficiency in achieving both short-term tasks and long-term goals.

ognitive Behavioral Techniques for Procrastina

6.1 Challenging Negative Thoughts

In the journey to overcome procrastination, understanding and addressing the role of negative thoughts is crucial. These thoughts often serve as the invisible barriers that keep individuals from initiating or completing tasks. The process of challenging negative thoughts is not just about dismissing them but involves a structured approach to question their validity, explore their origins, and replace them with more constructive and realistic perspectives.

Negative thoughts related to procrastination typically manifest in various forms such as self-doubt, fear of failure, perfectionism, or a lack of confidence in one's ability to successfully complete tasks. For instance, a thought like "I'm not smart enough to do this" not only undermines self-esteem but also reinforces avoidance behaviors. Challenging these thoughts requires individuals to first become aware of their presence and then critically assess them.

Identifying specific negative thoughts: Keeping a journal can help individuals track when they procrastinate and what negative thoughts accompany the behavior.

Questioning the evidence: This involves examining whether there is factual evidence supporting the negative thought or if it's based on unfounded fears or assumptions.

Considering alternative explanations: Often, there are other ways to view a situation that are less personal and more objective.

Reframing thoughts: This step focuses on replacing negative thoughts with more positive, yet realistic affirmations that encourage action rather than avoidance.

The effectiveness of challenging negative thoughts lies in its ability to shift one's mindset from being self-critical to becoming self-encouraging. For example, instead of thinking "I'll never be able to finish this on time," one could reframe it as "If I start now and work steadily, I can make significant progress." Such cognitive restructuring is not about fostering unrealistic optimism but about cultivating a more balanced and productive outlook towards tasks at hand.

Moreover, this technique empowers individuals by giving them control over their internal dialogue. It encourages a proactive rather than reactive response to procrastination triggers. By systematically dismantling the foundation upon which procrastination builds—

negative thought patterns—individuals can significantly enhance their motivation levels, improve task engagement, and reduce procrastination over time.

In conclusion, challenging negative thoughts is an essential cognitive behavioral technique for anyone looking to overcome procrastination. It not only aids in breaking the cycle of delay but also contributes to building resilience against future instances of procrastination by fostering a healthier mindset towards work and productivity.

6.2 Building a Positive Mindset

The journey from procrastination to productivity is not solely about managing time or organizing tasks; it fundamentally begins in the mind. Building a positive mindset is an essential step for individuals aiming to overcome procrastination. This process involves cultivating an attitude that encourages forward movement, resilience in the face of setbacks, and a belief in one's capabilities. A positive mindset does not mean ignoring challenges or pretending difficulties do not exist but rather approaching them with confidence and a constructive outlook.

A key aspect of building a positive mindset is learning to recognize and appreciate one's progress, no matter how small. This can significantly boost motivation and self-esteem, which are often eroded by chronic procrastination. For example, completing a small task on your to-do list or dedicating just 10 minutes towards a project you've been avoiding can be seen as victories worth celebrating. Such acknowledgments help shift focus from what hasn't been done to what has been accomplished, fostering a sense of achievement.

Another critical element is the practice of gratitude. By focusing on aspects of our lives and work that we are thankful for, we can counterbalance the often overwhelming feelings of dread or inadequacy that accompany procrastination. Gratitude helps in reframing our perspective towards our tasks and goals, making them seem less like insurmountable obstacles and more like opportunities for growth and satisfaction.

Moreover, visualization techniques serve as powerful tools in building a positive mindset. Envisioning oneself successfully completing tasks or achieving goals can create a mental blueprint for success, making the actual execution of tasks feel more attainable. Visualization not only aids in reducing anxiety associated with starting tasks but also enhances motivation by keeping the end goal vividly in mind.

In conclusion, building a positive mindset is pivotal for overcoming procrastination. It involves appreciating small successes, practicing gratitude, and employing visualization echniques to foster an environment where productivity can flourish. By shifting focus om negative thoughts to positive actions, individuals can break the cycle of rocrastination and move towards their goals with confidence and clarity.

6.3 Visualization and Affirmation Practices

The journey towards overcoming procrastination is significantly enhanced by ncorporating visualization and affirmation practices into one's daily routine. These ognitive behavioral techniques are powerful tools for reshaping one's mindset, fostering a ositive self-image, and ultimately driving productive behavior. By vividly imagining the uccessful completion of tasks and regularly affirming one's ability to overcome hallenges, individuals can create a mental environment conducive to action rather than voidance.

Visualization involves creating detailed mental images of achieving specific goals or ompleting tasks. This practice not only serves to demystify the process of reaching an bjective but also helps in building confidence by mentally rehearsing the steps needed for uccess. For instance, visualizing oneself organizing a workspace, engaging in focused ork sessions, or feeling the satisfaction of task completion can prime the mind for actual erformance. It bridges the gap between intention and action by making desired outcomes el more tangible and attainable.

Affirmations complement visualization by reinforcing positive beliefs about oneself and ne's capabilities through repeated verbal or written statements. These affirmations should e present-tense, positive assertions that counteract negative self-talk and doubts that often ccompany procrastination. Phrases like "I am capable of completing my tasks efficiently" r "I choose to focus on my goals with ease" are examples of affirmations that can shift indset from one of delay to one of determination.

Integrating visualization and affirmation practices into daily routines does not require xtensive time commitments but does call for consistency. Setting aside a few minutes each ay to engage in these practices can significantly impact one's approach to tasks and goals. hether it is through morning visualization exercises envisioning the day ahead or using firmations as breaks during work sessions, these techniques can serve as anchors keeping dividuals grounded in their intentions towards productivity.

In conclusion, visualization and affirmation practices are essential components in uilding a toolkit against procrastination. By harnessing the power of the mind to imagine success and affirm capabilities, individuals can alter their behavioral patterns towards greater efficiency and fulfillment. These practices not only aid in overcoming procrastination but also contribute to overall well-being by promoting a positive self-concept and resilience against setbacks.

7 Motivation and Reward Systems

7.1 Understanding Intrinsic vs Extrinsic Motivation

The distinction between intrinsic and extrinsic motivation is fundamental in the exploration of human behavior, particularly in the context of overcoming procrastination and enhancing productivity. This differentiation not only sheds light on why individuals engage in certain activities but also offers insights into how best to motivate oneself and others towards achieving personal and professional goals.

Intrinsic motivation refers to engaging in an activity for its inherent satisfaction rather than for some separable consequence. When intrinsically motivated, a person finds the task itself rewarding. For example, a writer might write because they find joy in crafting stories or expressing ideas creatively, not necessarily for fame or financial gain. This form of motivation is driven by internal desires such as curiosity, learning, personal challenge, or sheer enjoyment of the activity.

On the other hand, extrinsic motivation involves performing an activity to earn a reward or avoid punishment from external sources. The actions are not performed for their own sake but rather for obtaining something else or complying with external demands. Common examples include working a job primarily for the paycheck, studying hard to receive praise from parents or teachers, or exercising regularly to lose weight.

Understanding these two types of motivation is crucial because they have different effects on how people approach tasks and their level of persistence. Intrinsically motivated activities are more likely to be pursued with interest and are often associated with higher levels of creativity and satisfaction. Conversely, while extrinsic rewards can effectively motivate people to perform a task they might not otherwise engage in, this type of motivation may diminish if the rewards stop or if the task becomes unchallenging.

Moreover, research suggests that over-reliance on extrinsic rewards can sometimes undermine intrinsic motivation—a phenomenon known as the "overjustification effect." For instance, if an individual who enjoys painting starts doing it solely for commercial success, they may begin to find the activity less enjoyable when done without financial incentive.

In conclusion, recognizing whether one's motivation is intrinsic or extrinsic can offer valuable insights into managing procrastination and improving productivity. It highlights the importance of finding personal meaning and enjoyment in tasks as a way to sustain engagement and performance over time. Additionally, understanding these motivational drivers can aid individuals and organizations in designing more effective motivational strategies that align with desired outcomes.

7.2 Designing Effective Reward Systems

Designing effective reward systems is a critical component in fostering both intrinsic and extrinsic motivation within an organization or any setting where performance and productivity are key. The essence of a well-structured reward system lies in its ability to align the objectives of the individual with those of the organization, thereby promoting a culture of achievement and recognition.

The first step in designing an effective reward system is understanding the diverse needs and motivations of the individuals involved. This require a deep dive into what drives people beyond surface-level incentives, tapping into their intrinsic desires for mastery, connection, autonomy, and purpose. By integrating these psychological drivers into the reward system rganizations can create more meaningful and motivating rewards that esonate on a personal level with their employees or team members.

Another crucial aspect is ensuring that the rewards are perceived as fair nd equitable. Equity theory suggests that individuals assess the fairness of heir work outcomes in relation to others. Therefore, transparent criteria for arning rewards must be established to avoid feelings of injustice that could ndermine motivation. This involves setting clear, achievable goals and ommunicating how rewards are linked to specific performances or chievements.

Customization of rewards to fit individual preferences and values

Regular feedback loops to adjust and improve the reward system over ime

Incorporation of non-monetary rewards such as recognition programs, rofessional development opportunities, or additional autonomy in job roles

Beyond individual rewards, designing systems that foster team-based ncentives can also enhance collaboration and collective effort towards ommon goals. This approach not only strengthens team dynamics but also everages peer recognition as a powerful motivator.

In conclusion, an effective reward system is multifaceted; it must be houghtfully designed with an understanding of human psychology at its ore. It should balance between extrinsic incentives like pay raises or onuses with intrinsic motivators such as personal growth opportunities or neaningful work contributions. By doing so, organizations can cultivate an nvironment where motivation thrives, leading to sustained engagement and roductivity.

7.3 Maintaining Long-Term Motivation

Maintaining long-term motivation within an organization or team is a complex, ongoing process that requires more than just the initial spark of excitement or the promise of rewards. It involves creating an environment where individuals feel continuously inspired, valued, and connected to their work and the broader organizational goals. This enduring motivation is crucial for achieving sustained high performance and productivity over time.

To foster long-term motivation, it's essential to understand that what motivates individuals can evolve. Early career professionals might be driven by opportunities for learning and growth, whereas more experienced employees may value autonomy or the ability to mentor others. Recognizing and adapting to these shifting motivations is key to maintaining engagement across different stages of an individual's career.

Another critical aspect is the role of meaningful work. When people see how their efforts contribute to a larger purpose or make a tangible difference in the world, they are more likely to remain motivated over the long haul. This sense of purpose can be cultivated through clear communication about organizational goals, celebrating achievements that contribute to these objectives, and connecting day-to-day tasks with overarching missions.

Implementing flexible reward systems that can evolve with employees' changing needs and motivations

Encouraging a culture of continuous learning and development

Fostering strong relationships within teams and across the organization

Providing regular feedback that recognizes contributions while also offering constructive guidance for growth

Beyond individual factors, creating a supportive community within the workplace plays a significant role in sustaining motivation. When employees feel part of a team where their contributions are recognized and they can rely on others for support, it enhances their commitment and drive. Building this sense of community involves not only formal mechanisms like team-building activities but also fostering an everyday culture of respect, inclusion, and collaboration.

In conclusion, maintaining long-term motivation requires a multifaceted approach that goes beyond simple reward systems. It demands attention to evolving motivations, fostering meaningful work, encouraging continuous development, building strong relationships, and cultivating a supportive community culture. By addressing these areas thoughtfully and consistently, organizations can create an environment where motivation endures and flourishes.

Breaking Down Tasks into Manageable Ste

8.1 The Art of Task Segmentation

In the journey to overcome procrastination and enhance productivity, mastering the art of task segmentation stands as a pivotal strategy. This approach not only simplifies complex tasks but also significantly reduces the overwhelming feeling that often leads to procrastination. By breaking down tasks into smaller, more manageable steps, individuals can tackle their responsibilities with greater clarity and focus, paving the way for a more organized and efficient workflow.

Task segmentation operates on the principle that large projects are more approachable when divided into smaller pieces. This division makes it easier to start working on a project since each segment feels less daunting than facing the entire task at once. Moreover, completing these smaller segments provides a sense of accomplishment and progress, which serves as motivation to continue moving forward. This psychological boost is crucial in maintaining momentum and avoiding the stagnation that often accompanies procrastination.

To effectively implement task segmentation, one must first understand the scope of the project at hand. This involves identifying all necessary components and determining a logical order for addressing each part. Once this overview is established, individuals can begin to allocate specific time frames for completing each segment, taking care to set realistic deadlines that reflect their capacity and available resources.

In conclusion, embracing the art of task segmentation equips individuals with a powerful tool against procrastination. It breaks down barriers of fear and overwhelm by presenting a clear path forward through any project or goal. As such, mastering this technique is essential for anyone looking to enhance their productivity and achieve their objectives with confidence and efficiency.

Identify the overall goal of your project or task.

Break down this goal into major components or milestones.

Divide these components further into actionable steps or tasks.

Prioritize these tasks based on urgency and importance.

Allocate time blocks for focusing on each task individually.

The effectiveness of task segmentation lies in its flexibility; it can be applied across various contexts, from academic assignments to complex professional projects. By tailoring this strategy to fit personal work habits and preferences, individuals can transform their approach to tasks from one of dread and avoidance to one characterized by control and proactive engagement. Furthermore, this method fosters better planning and time management skills, contributing to long-term success in overcoming procrastination.

8.2 Using Micro-Goals for Macro Success

The concept of micro-goals plays a crucial role in the broader strategy of task segmentation, serving as the bridge between planning and execution. By setting small, achievable objectives, individuals can create a step-by-step roadmap towards accomplishing larger goals. This method not only simplifies complex projects but also instills a sense of progress and achievement, which is essential for maintaining motivation and momentum.

Micro-goals work by breaking down overarching objectives into bite-sized tasks that can be completed within a short timeframe. This approach makes daunting projects feel more manageable and less intimidating. For instance, writing a book—a seemingly monumental task—can be divided into daily word count targets, making the process more digestible and less overwhelming.

Moreover, micro-goals offer immediate feedback on one's progress. Completing these smaller tasks provides tangible evidence of advancement towards the larger goal, which can significantly boost morale and motivation. This continuous cycle of setting and achieving micro-goals creates a positive feedback loop that propels individuals forward, keeping procrastination at bay.

Another advantage of using micro-goals is their flexibility. They allow for adjustments based on performance and unforeseen challenges without derailing the overall project. If an individual falls short on a daily goal, they can reassess and recalibrate their efforts for the next day without losing sight of the ultimate objective.

To effectively implement micro-goals, it's important to ensure that they are specific, measurable, achievable, relevant, and time-bound (SMART). This criterion ensures that each goal serves as an effective stepping stone towards larger achievements. Additionally, celebrating the completion of micro-goals can serve as an effective motivational tool. Acknowledging these small wins reinforces positive behavior and keeps individuals engaged in their work.

In conclusion, integrating micro-goals into one's workflow is a powerful technique for enhancing productivity and achieving success in any endeavor. By transforming large projects into a series of manageable tasks, individuals can navigate through complex challenges with greater ease and confidence. The cumulative effect of these small victories paves the way for significant accomplishments over time.

8.3 Dealing with Overwhelming Projects

When faced with a project that seems insurmountable, the initial reaction can often be one of stress or avoidance. However, by applying strategic approaches to break down the enormity of the task at hand, these overwhelming projects can become more approachable and less daunting. This section delves into methods for dissecting large projects into manageable segments, thereby transforming anxiety into actionable steps.

The first step in tackling an overwhelming project is to conduct a comprehensive assessment of its scope and requirements. This involves identifying all components of the project and understanding their interrelations. By doing so, you can gain a clearer picture of what needs to be accomplished and prioritize tasks based on their importance and urgency.

Following this, employing the concept of micro-goals—similar to those discussed in the context of enhancing productivity through task segmentation—becomes crucial. Micro-goals allow for the division of a large project into smaller, nore manageable tasks that can be completed within a reasonable timeframe. For example, if the project involves developing a new software application, one could set daily or weekly goals focusing on writing specific amounts of code or completing individual modules.

Another effective strategy is to allocate dedicated time blocks for focused work on each segment of the project. This technique, known as time boxing, helps prevent procrastination and ensures steady progress is made towards completion. It also allows for regular breaks to refresh and maintain high levels of productivity over extended periods.

Maintaining flexibility throughout the process is also key. Unforeseen challenges may arise that necessitate adjustments to your plan or timeline. Being prepared to reassess and recalibrate your approach when needed can help keep the project moving forward without becoming overwhelmed by setbacks.

Lastly, it's important not to underestimate the power of seeking support when dealing with overwhelming projects. Collaborating with colleagues or reaching out for expert advice can provide new insights and solutions that simplify complex problems. Additionally, sharing progress with others can offer motivation and encouragement to continue pushing through difficult phases.

In conclusion, transforming an overwhelming project into a series of manageable tasks requires thorough planning, strategic goal setting, dedicated focus periods, adaptability in response to challenges, and openness to collaboration. By applying these principles diligently, what once seemed like an insurmountable challenge can gradually become an achievable objective.

Developing Resilience Against Procrastinati

9.1 Embracing Imperfection

In the journey to overcome procrastination, embracing imperfection emerges as a pivotal step. This concept is not merely about accepting that we are not perfect; it's about understanding how the pursuit of perfection itself can be a profound source of delay and inaction. The fear of failing or not meeting high standards can paralyze individuals, making the task at hand seem so daunting that it's easier to postpone than to face head-on.

The idea of embracing imperfection is rooted in the understanding that progress, rather than perfection, should be the goal. It challenges the all-or-nothing mindset that often accompanies procrastination. For instance, a student might avoid starting a paper thinking it needs to be flawless from the outset, rather than drafting ideas and refining them over time. Similarly, professionals may delay projects due to concerns over every detail being perfect, missing opportunities for growth and feedback in the process.

Embracing imperfection involves several key strategies:

Setting realistic goals: Understanding that perfection is unattainable and setting achievable targets instead.

Focusing on progress: Celebrating small victories and incremental progress towards larger objectives.

Reframing failure: Viewing mistakes not as failures but as learning opportunities and stepping stones to success.

Practicing self-compassion: Being kind to oneself when things don't go as planned instead of resorting to self-criticism which can fuel further procrastination.

This shift in perspective is crucial for overcoming procrastination. By accepting that imperfections are part of being human and focusing on moving forward despite them, individuals can break the cycle of delay. It allows for a more flexible approach to tasks and goals, reducing the pressure that leads to procrastination. Moreover, embracing imperfection encourages a healthier relationship with work and personal goals by prioritizing learning and growth over unattainable ideals.

In conclusion, embracing imperfection is not about lowering standards but about redefining what success looks like. It's about making peace with the fact that mistakes will happen and that there's beauty in the effort and resilience shown in facing challenges head-on. This mindset is essential for anyone looking to develop resilience against procrastination and unlock their full potential.

9.2 Learning from Setbacks

After embracing imperfection, the next crucial step in developing resilience against procrastination is learning from setbacks. This phase is about understanding that setbacks are not just obstacles but invaluable opportunities for growth and self-improvement. It's a shift from viewing failures as end points to seeing them as integral parts of the journey towards achieving our goals.

When we procrastinate, we often do so out of fear of failure or making mistakes. However, by reframing how we perceive these setbacks, we can lessen the grip of procrastination on our lives. Instead of allowing a setback to reinforce our desire to delay tasks further, we can use it as a catalyst for reflection and future action.

Learning from setbacks involves several key approaches:

Analyzing the setback: Taking a step back to understand what led to the setback, without resorting to self-criticism. This could involve identifying specific actions that didn't work out as planned or recognizing external factors that were out of our control.

Adapting strategies: Based on the analysis, determining what can be done differently next time. This might mean adjusting timelines, seeking additional resources or support, or changing tactics altogether.

Maintaining perspective: Recognizing that most successful people have faced and overcome numerous setbacks. What often sets them apart is their ability to persevere and learn from these experiences rather than being derailed by them.

Celebrating progress: Acknowledging any progress made towards goals, even if it wasn't as much as hoped for. This helps build momentum and keeps motivation alive.

This process not only aids in overcoming procrastination but also contributes to personal growth by enhancing problem-solving skills and emotional resilience. By learning from setbacks instead of fearing them, individuals can develop a more proactive approach to tasks and challenges. This mindset shift is essential for anyone looking to break free from the cycle of delay and achieve their full potential.

In conclusion, learning from setbacks is about harnessing the lessons embedded within every failure or mistake. It encourages a constructive response to challenges and fosters an environment where continuous improvement is possible. Embracing this approach can significantly reduce procrastination by transforming fear into action and setbacks into stepping stones towards success.

9.3 Cultivating Grit and Determination

The journey from procrastination to productivity is not just about managing time or tasks; it's fundamentally about cultivating an inner resilience that can weather the storms of setbacks and failures. This resilience is built on the twin pillars of grit and determination. Grit, as defined by psychologist Angela Duckworth, is the power of passion and perseverance toward long-term goals. Determination, similarly, involves a steadfastness towards achieving one's objectives despite difficulties. Together, they form a formidable defense against the tendency to procrastinate.

Grit enables individuals to maintain their focus and effort over extended periods, even when immediate rewards are not evident. It's about having an enduring commitment to your goals, which transcends daily fluctuations in motivation or enthusiasm. Determination complements grit by providing the tenacity required to push through challenges and setbacks without giving up.

To cultivate grit and determination, one must first embrace a growth mindset—the belief that abilities can be developed through dedication and hard work. This perspective encourages viewing challenges as opportunities to grow rather than insurmountable obstacles. Furthermore, setting clear, meaningful goals provides direction for sustained effort and helps maintain motivation over time.

Building resilience against procrastination also involves developing robust habits that support consistent action towards your goals. This includes establishing routines that prioritize important tasks, breaking down larger projects into manageable steps, and creating a supportive environment that minimizes distractions.

Another key aspect of cultivating grit and determination is learning how to effectively manage failure. Instead of allowing setbacks to derail progress, resilient individuals analyze what went wrong, adjust their strategies accordingly, and persist in their efforts with renewed vigor.

In conclusion, overcoming procrastination requires more than just good time management skills; it demands the cultivation of deep-seated qualities like grit and determination. By fostering these attributes within ourselves, we can develop the resilience needed to pursue our goals relentlessly—transforming procrastination into productivity through sheer force of will.

Technology and Tools to Combat Procrastinat

10.1 Digital Tools for Time Management

In the quest to conquer procrastination, digital tools for time management play a pivotal role. These applications and platforms are designed not just to remind us of our tasks but to structure our days, prioritize activities, and visualize progress. In an era where distractions are just a click away, these digital solutions offer a structured approach to managing time effectively, thereby directly addressing one of the root causes of procrastination.

The importance of these tools cannot be overstated in today's fast-paced environment. They serve as personal assistants that help users allocate their most limited resource—time—more judiciously. From simple to-do lists that keep track of daily tasks to complex project management software that plans out months or even years in advance, these tools cater to a wide range of needs and preferences.

Digital tools for time management not only assist in planning out tasks but also provide insights into how one spends their time. Many apps feature reporting capabilities that allow users to review their productivity patterns over weeks or months. This feedback loop is crucial for identifying areas of improvement and adjusting strategies accordingly. Moreover, integrating these tools across devices ensures that reminders follow you wherever you go, making it harder to overlook responsibilities.

In conclusion, leveraging digital tools for time management is an effective strategy against procrastination. By providing structure and visibility into how we allocate our time, these applications empower us to take control over our schedules and ultimately our lives. As we become more intentional about how we spend each hour of our day, we can reduce procrastination significantly and move closer towards achieving our personal and professional goals.

Task Management Apps: Applications like Todoist, Microsoft To Do, and Trello allow users to create tasks, set deadlines, and categorize work into different projects or aspects of life. Their intuitive interfaces make it easy for anyone to start organizing their life more efficiently.

Time Blocking Software: Tools such as Google Calendar or Outlook provide functionalities beyond mere scheduling. They enable time blocking—a method where every hour of the day is assigned a specific task or activity, thus minimizing wasted time and enhancing focus.

Pomodoro Timers: Based on the Pomodoro Technique, apps like Be Focused offer a simple yet effective way to manage working hours by breaking them into intervals (traditionally 25 minutes), separated by short breaks. This promotes sustained concentration and prevents burnout.

Habit Tracking Apps: For those looking to build productive habits or break unhelpful ones, habit trackers such as Habitica gamify the process, making it fun and engaging to stick with new routines.

10.2 Apps for Focus and Productivity

In the digital age, where distractions are omnipresent, maintaining focus and enhancing productivity has become a significant challenge. This is where apps designed specifically to boost concentration and efficiency come into play. Unlike general time management tools that primarily assist in scheduling and task organization, focus and productivity apps delve deeper into the mechanics of work habits, offering solutions tailored to overcoming procrastination and fostering a productive mindset.

One of the most popular methodologies incorporated by these apps is the Pomodoro Technique, which breaks down work into intervals, traditionally 25 minutes in length, followed by short breaks. This method not only encourages deep focus but also ensures regular rest periods to prevent burnout. Apps like *Focus Booster* and *Pomotodo* take this approach, integrating task management with the Pomodoro timer to provide a comprehensive productivity system.

Beyond time management, certain apps aim to minimize distractions by blocking access to websites and apps that may lure users away from their work. *Freedom* and *Cold Turkey* are examples of such software, allowing individuals to create customized lists of distractions that can be temporarily blocked across various devices. This ensures that during work sessions, the temptation to drift off into non-work-related activities is significantly reduced.

Mind mapping tools like *MindMeister*

offer another dimension to productivity by helping users organize thoughts and ideas
visually. These applications support brainstorming sessions, project planning, and note-
taking in a more interactive manner than traditional linear notes do. By providing a
visual overview of tasks or ideas, mind mapping can enhance clarity and facilitate more
efficient problem-solving.

To address the issue of motivation—a common barrier to productivity—some apps
incorporate gamification elements into their design. Habitica, for instance, turns daily
tasks and goals into a role-playing game where completing real-life tasks results in
rewards for one's avatar within the app. This blend of entertainment with productivity
provides an engaging way to stay on track with personal or professional objectives.

In conclusion, focusing on specific aspects such as minimizing distractions, managing energy levels through timed work sessions, organizing thoughts visually, or even gamifying tasks can significantly impact one's ability to maintain concentration and achieve higher levels of productivity. As these apps continue to evolve with advancements in technology and psychology research findings being integrated into their functionalities—they represent vital tools in the modern individual's arsenal against procrastination.

10.3 Blocking Distractions in the Digital Age

In an era where digital distractions are just a click away, finding effective strategies to block these interruptions is crucial for maintaining focus and productivity. The constant availability of social media, streaming services, and instant messaging apps can significantly hinder one's ability to concentrate on tasks at hand. Recognizing this challenge, various tools and technologies have been developed to assist individuals in creating a distraction-free digital environment.

Software solutions like *Freedom* and *Cold Turkey* offer robust features that allow users to block distracting websites and applications across multiple devices. These tools are designed not only to prevent access during specified times but also to customize the level of restriction based on individual needs. For instance, someone might block all social media during work hours while allowing access to music streaming services that don't hamper productivity.

Beyond blocking specific sites or apps, there are browser extensions such as *StayFocusd* that limit the amount of time spent on distraction-prone websites. This approach acknowledges that while complete avoidance of certain digital spaces is unrealistic for some, moderating the time spent on them can still significantly enhance focus.

The integration of scheduling features within these tools plays a pivotal role in managing distractions effectively. By allowing users to set up focused sessions ahead of time, it becomes easier to adhere to planned work periods without succumbing to the lure of digital temptations. Moreover, some applications provide analytics on usage patterns, offering insights into which activities consume the most time and how changes in behavior impact productivity.

An emerging trend in combating digital distractions involves leveraging technology not just as a barrier but as a motivator. Gamification elements found in apps like *Habitica* reward users for sticking with their focus goals, turning the challenge of avoiding distractions into an engaging game-like experience.

In conclusion, as we navigate through the complexities of the digital age, having access to tools that can effectively block out distractions is invaluable. Whether through website blockers, browser extensions with time limits, or gamified productivity apps, these technologies empower individuals to reclaim control over their attention span and enhance their capacity for deep work.

11 Creating a Supportive Environment

11.1 Building Accountability Partnerships

In the journey to overcome procrastination and enhance productivity, establishing accountability partnerships stands out as a pivotal strategy. This approach leverages the power of mutual commitment to foster a supportive environment where individuals can thrive. Accountability partnerships are not merely about checking off tasks; they are about building a relationship grounded in trust, encouragement, and shared goals.

The essence of an accountability partnership lies in its ability to transform the daunting path of personal improvement into a shared venture. When two or more people come together with the intention of holding each other accountable, they create a dynamic space that is conducive to growth and change. This collaborative effort helps in breaking down tasks into manageable chunks, setting realistic deadlines, and providing the necessary motivation to stay on track.

One of the key benefits of accountability partnerships is the external perspective that partners bring to each other's goals and challenges. Often, when we are too close to our own situations, it becomes difficult to see potential solutions or recognize patterns of procrastination. An accountability partner can offer fresh insights, suggest alternative approaches, and help identify blind spots that may be hindering progress.

Beyond these practical steps, building an accountability partnership also involves cultivating empathy and understanding. Recognizing that setbacks are part of the process allows both partners to support each other through challenges without judgment. Celebrating successes, no matter how small, boosts morale and reinforces positive behavior towards achieving long-term goals.

Regular Check-ins: Establishing routine meetings or check-ins (whether virtual or in-person) ensures ongoing communication and reinforces commitment to shared objectives.

Goal Setting: Collaboratively setting clear, achievable goals provides direction and fosters a sense of purpose within the partnership.

Feedback Loop: Constructive feedback is crucial for growth. Partners should feel comfortable offering honest feedback and receiving it with openness.

In conclusion, building accountability partnerships offers a robust framework for overcoming procrastination by harnessing the collective strength of collaboration. By committing to support one another's journey towards productivity, individuals can unlock their full potential and achieve their aspirations more effectively than going it alone.

11.2 Seeking Professional Help When Needed

In the journey towards personal improvement and productivity, there comes a point where the support from accountability partners might need to be supplemented with professional guidance. Recognizing when to seek professional help is crucial in navigating challenges that go beyond the scope of mutual accountability partnerships. This step is not about admitting defeat but rather about acknowledging the complexity of human behavior and the benefits of specialized intervention.

Professional help can come in various forms, including counseling, coaching, or therapy, each offering unique approaches to overcoming procrastination and enhancing productivity. These professionals bring a wealth of knowledge and techniques grounded in research and clinical practice, tailored to address individual needs and circumstances. For instance, cognitive-behavioral therapy (CBT) has been shown to be particularly effective in tackling procrastination by helping individuals identify and challenge unhelpful thought patterns and behaviors.

Seeking professional help also provides a confidential space to explore underlying issues that may contribute to procrastination, such as anxiety, depression, or ADHD. These conditions can significantly impact one's ability to stay motivated and complete tasks. A professional can offer strategies for managing these challenges while working towards greater productivity. Moreover, they can provide objective feedback and insights that are difficult to obtain from peers or self-reflection alone.

The decision to seek professional help should be viewed as a proactive step towards self-improvement. It demonstrates a commitment to overcoming obstacles by leveraging all available resources. Importantly, it also contributes to destigmatizing mental health support in contexts related to work and personal development.

In conclusion, while accountability partnerships offer valuable support in overcoming procrastination, recognizing when professional intervention is needed represents an advanced level of self-awareness and commitment to personal growth. By embracing both peer support and professional guidance, individuals can create a comprehensive approach that addresses both surface-level behaviors and deeper psychological factors contributing to procrastination.

11.3 Fostering a Community of Productivity

In the pursuit of personal and professional growth, fostering a community of productivity stands as a pivotal strategy. This approach not only amplifies individual efforts but also cultivates an environment where collective success is celebrated. The essence of creating such a community lies in understanding the symbiotic relationship between motivation, collaboration, and shared goals.

The foundation of a productive community is built on mutual respect and the recognition that every member has unique strengths and insights to offer. Encouraging open communication and regular feedback sessions can significantly enhance this dynamic. These practices ensure that all voices are heard, fostering a sense of belonging and commitment among members.

Another critical aspect involves setting clear, achievable goals. When individuals understand how their contributions fit into the larger picture, they are more likely to stay motivated and engaged. Establishing these objectives also provides a framework for accountability, allowing members to support each other in overcoming obstacles and celebrating milestones.

Moreover, leveraging technology can play an instrumental role in maintaining connectivity within the community. Digital tools and platforms offer innovative ways to collaborate, share resources, and track progress towards common goals. They also enable flexibility in how members engage with one another, accommodating diverse schedules and working styles.

However, it's important to recognize that fostering a productive community goes beyond merely achieving tasks; it's about nurturing growth and development at both the individual and collective levels. Providing opportunities for learning—such as workshops, seminars, or mentorship programs—can enrich the community experience further. These initiatives not only enhance skills but also reinforce the value of continuous improvement.

In conclusion, creating a community of productivity requires intentional effort across multiple dimensions: communication, goal-setting, technology use, and development opportunities. By prioritizing these elements, leaders can cultivate an environment where everyone thrives together—a space where productivity blossoms from shared purpose and mutual support.

2 Sustaining Progress and Preventing Relap

12.1 Monitoring Progress Through Journaling

In the journey to overcome procrastination and enhance productivity, monitoring progress plays a pivotal role. Journaling emerges as a powerful tool in this context, offering individuals a structured way to track their achievements, reflect on their setbacks, and understand the nuances of their behavior patterns over time. This method not only aids in recognizing how far one has come but also in identifying specific areas that require more focus or a different approach.

Journaling for progress involves more than merely noting down tasks completed or postponed; it encompasses a comprehensive reflection on the emotional and psychological aspects of one's productivity journey. By regularly documenting thoughts, feelings, successes, and challenges, individuals gain deeper insights into the triggers of procrastination and the effectiveness of strategies employed to combat it. This reflective practice encourages a mindset shift from being task-oriented to growth-oriented, where the emphasis is on continuous improvement rather than mere completion of tasks.

The act of journaling itself can transform into a ritual that fosters discipline—a crucial antidote to procrastination. Moreover, by serving as an accountability partner to oneself, journaling creates a sense of responsibility towards personal growth goals. Over time, this habit not only aids in combating procrastination but also contributes significantly to personal development and self-awareness.

In conclusion, monitoring progress through journaling is an invaluable strategy within the broader framework of overcoming procrastination. It offers nuanced insights into one's behavioral patterns while providing a structured mechanism for self-reflection and strategy optimization. As such, incorporating journaling into one's daily routine can significantly enhance the journey towards sustained productivity and success.

Setting clear goals: Journal entries should begin with articulating specific, measurable objectives for what one hopes to achieve within a set timeframe. This clarity serves as a roadmap guiding daily actions and decisions.

Recording daily accomplishments: Noting down tasks accomplished each day provides immediate satisfaction and reinforces positive behavior. It also helps in visualizing progress over time.

Analyzing setbacks: Equally important is reflecting on days when goals were not met. Understanding the reasons behind procrastination episodes can unveil patterns and triggers that need addressing.

Adjusting strategies: Based on reflections, individuals can tweak their approaches to overcoming procrastination. Journaling thus becomes an iterative process of learning and adaptation.

12.2 Adjusting Strategies as Needed

The journey towards overcoming procrastination and enhancing productivity is not a linear path; it requires constant evaluation and adjustment of strategies to ensure sustained progress. The act of journaling, as discussed in the previous section, lays a solid foundation for this process by providing insights into personal productivity patterns, successes, and setbacks. However, recognizing the need for change is only the first step. Implementing effective adjustments to one's approach is crucial for moving forward.

Adjusting strategies as needed involves a deep dive into the reflections captured through journaling. It demands an honest assessment of what's working and what isn't. This could mean altering time management techniques, experimenting with new productivity tools, or even redefining goals to better align with one's current capabilities and circumstances. The essence of this process lies in its flexibility— being open to change and willing to experiment with different methods until finding what best suits one's unique workflow.

For instance, if journal entries consistently highlight distractions as a major cause of procrastination, one might explore strategies such as the Pomodoro Technique for better focus management or digital tools that limit access to distracting websites during work hours. Similarly, if reflections reveal a pattern of energy dips at certain times of the day affecting productivity, adjusting one's schedule to tackle high-priority tasks during peak energy levels could be beneficial.

Moreover, adjusting strategies is not solely about rectifying shortcomings; it also encompasses scaling successful tactics. If journaling uncovers particular habits or routines that significantly boost productivity, efforts should be made to reinforce these practices and integrate them more deeply into one's daily life.

In conclusion, adjusting strategies as needed is a dynamic process that plays a pivotal role in sustaining progress towards overcoming procrastination and achieving personal growth goals. It requires an iterative approach of trial and error, guided by self-reflection through journaling. By staying adaptable and responsive to their evolving needs and challenges, individuals can continuously refine their strategies for enhanced productivity and success.

12.3 Celebrating Milestones

Celebrating milestones is a crucial component in the journey towards overcoming procrastination and enhancing productivity. It serves not only as a form of recognition for the hard work and progress made but also as a motivational tool that encourages continued effort and dedication. Recognizing and celebrating each achievement, no matter how small, reinforces positive behavior and fosters a sense of accomplishment.

When individuals set goals, they embark on a path that is often challenging and requires persistent effort. Reaching milestones along this path can provide tangible evidence of progress, making the ultimate goal seem more attainable. Celebrations act as checkpoints that remind individuals of how far they have come, which is particularly important during moments of doubt or when facing obstacles.

The act of celebrating can vary greatly from person to person; it might involve taking some time off to relax, sharing achievements with friends or family, or treating oneself to something special. The key is to acknowledge the effort put into reaching that milestone in a way that feels rewarding and meaningful to the individual.

Moreover, celebrating milestones can also serve as an opportunity for reflection. It allows individuals to look back on the journey thus far, evaluate the strategies that have been effective, and consider adjustments for future challenges. This reflective process not only enhances self-awareness but also contributes to personal growth by highlighting strengths and areas for improvement.

In addition to personal celebrations, sharing achievements with peers or mentors can provide an added layer of validation and support. Social recognition can boost confidence and inspire others in their pursuits, creating a positive feedback loop within communities or teams working towards similar goals.

In conclusion, celebrating milestones is more than just a reward; it's an integral part of sustaining momentum towards achieving long-term goals. By acknowledging each step forward, individuals reinforce their commitment to personal growth and productivity while cultivating a mindset that values progress over perfection.

"Overcoming Procrastination: A Step-by-Step Guide" addresses the widespread issue of procrastination, which impedes personal and professional growth in today's fast-paced environment. With a significant portion of the population admitting to procrastinating, this non-fiction book targets individuals who struggle with delaying tasks and managing time effectively. It aims to dissect the psychology behind procrastination and provide practical strategies for overcoming it, making it relevant for students, professionals, and anyone looking to enhance productivity.

The book is divided into two main sections for clarity and ease of application. The first part explores the root causes of procrastination, including fear of failure, perfectionism, and lack of motivation. It draws on recent research and insights from psychology experts to offer readers a deep understanding of why they procrastinate. The second section presents a collection of strategies and techniques to tackle procrastination directly. These include time management hacks, goal-setting frameworks, and cognitive behavioral techniques aimed at reshaping one's mindset towards productivity.

Emphasizing practicality, "Overcoming Procrastination: A Step-by-Step Guide" combines theoretical knowledge with real-life examples and interactive exercises. This approach ensures that readers can relate to the content personally while learning how to apply these strategies in their lives. The book not only seeks to inspire temporary motivation but also aims to instill lasting habits for long-term success and fulfillment. It serves as an invaluable resource for anyone wishing to reclaim control over their time and actions by mastering the art of productivity.

Made in United States
Troutdale, OR
04/24/2025

30873097R00037